For L
With

MW00396555

/

foot

SPECKS
AND
FLASHES

Poems by
Robert H. Deluty

GATEWAY PRESS, INC.
Baltimore, MD   2006

Please direct all correspondence and book orders to:
Robert H. Deluty
4783 Ilkley Moor Lane
Ellicott City, Maryland 21043

Library of Congress Control Number 2006921834
ISBN 0-9704201-9-6

Published by
Gateway Press, Inc.
3600 Clipper Mill Rd., Suite 260
Baltimore, MD 21211-1953

Printed in the United States of America

To
Joseph Masling, Kenneth Maton,
Leon Levy, Dorothy McLaughlin,
Joseph DeVitis, Kenneth Levy,
Arlene Burrows, Aron Siegman,
Thomas Burns, Jonathan Finkelstein,
Phyllis Walsh, and Gerald Patterson

Other books by Robert H. Deluty
published by Gateway Press

Within and Between: Poems (2000)
The Long and Short of It: Essays and Poems (2003)
Observed and Imagined: Poems and Essays (2004)
The Essence of Moments: Poems (2004)
Treasuring the Details: Poems (2005)
Present Sense: New and Selected Poems (2005)
Glimpses and Snapshots: Poems (2005)

Contents

8   his four daughters
chemo patient smiles
two-year-old twins
bus terminal
a day off from school

9   family photo
first trip to Brooklyn
post-liposuction
faculty meeting
grieving five-year-old

10   November 1st
Christmas morning
mortified mother
their three-year-old
April Fool's Day

11   her three grandsons
elderly man
Thanksgiving dinner
senile ex-sailor
newly licensed teen

12   polygamist
under their sofa
sweltering June day
centenarian
asking her rabbi

13   physics professor
hotel lobby
a hungry child
next-door neighbors
white supremacist

23 *It's a boy*
   peewee football coach
   nursing home supper
   bipolar teen
   after the nightmare

24 his son resolves
   commemorating
   at 5 a.m.
   pre-turkey dinner
   Jewish boy asking

25 from the bathroom
   a man at the bank
   crowded metro
   senryu writer
   his three-year-old son

26 post-hurricane
   before dining
   seated in long rows
   widow wondering
   Yom Kippur, midday

27 teenager's father
   his third wife
   four-year-old girl
   between clients
   remembering Mom

28 sends back the soup
   twin boys in the tub
   police officer
   blue jay squawking
   tenement child

29   job candidate
       Malibu teen
       at *Kohl's*
       travel agent
       U.S. senator

30   white-haired since '90
       adoptive father
       psychoanalyst
       their son arguing
       OCD child

31   veteran teacher
       her homework untouched
       paperless poet
       faculty retreat
       a baby carriage

32   newspaper obit
       her gay uncle
       his new patient
       first-year resident
       ten-month-old baby

33   alarming increase
       psychotic Jew
       first day of school
       inner city
       freshman's parents

34   infirm old man
       her coloring book
       internist's office
       on Thanksgiving
       senile ex-teacher

44 breast-feeding mother
   Russian weightlifter
   porn actress
   atop Santa's lap
   longtime waitress

45 three-year-old boy
   state spelling bee
   depressed dieter
   lying in traction
   a Jew makes peace

46 truck stop restroom
   psychotherapist
   prison inmate
   driving instructor
   masquerade party

47 a cell phone rings
   city bakery
   last-second shot
   her son, looking pained
   sick of footnotes

48 NBA all-star
   college gymnast
   beauty parlor
   immigrant's young son
   his first grad student

49 irate poet
   his pre-teen daughters
   first retirement check
   new superhero
   science teacher

50   lymphoma patient
       newly licensed
       beleaguered father
       an actuary
       high school daredevil

51   watching a porn film
       public golf course
       off-Broadway
       a two-year-old boy
       defensive tackle

52   a street mime
       job interviewee
       sullen professor
       Super Bowl eve
       five-year-old hunter

53   Reality

54   a colleague asking
       army private
       construction worker
       an errant pass
       four-year-old Jew

55   young academic
       nudist beach
       Boston professor
       pro athlete
       dining out

56   to his priest
       a revered rabbi
       thirty years after
       a drunk driver
       on line at *Starbucks*

Specks and Flashes

As with Blake, haiku poets see the universe in a grain of sand; they suggest an entire astronomy by their specks and flashes.

Robert Spiess

seventh heaven ...
after six miscarriages,
a healthy baby

Halloween night ...
sleeping on a pillow case
filled with chocolates

geography class ...
a late student is given
no latitude

doctoral student
singing Gospel hymns
before her orals

cross-country trucker
battling fog, fatigue, and
four frankfurters

elderly tutor
offering the eulogy
for his first pupil

Thanksgiving night ...
five girlfriends discussing
turkeys they've known

Fenway in April ...
a Sox fan wearing earmuffs
under his cap

mid-argument
his young Protestant stepson
calling him *Jewboy*

their first session ...
a psychiatrist staring
at a teen's acne

deathbed confession ...
a vegan spokesman admits
to loving chicken

rapt teenaged Goth
glued to his television
watching bass fishing

old woman sleeping ...
her grandsons peeling the skin
from her sunburned arms

floral photographs
and haiku adorn the walls
of her prison cell

fall equinox ...
his daughter changing
her hair color

vanity plate
on a new Mercedes:
AYNRAND

old man's wallet …
fraying photographs
of his four ex-wives

ex-ballerina
teaching her palsied daughter
how to dance

funeral parlor …
their young son making faces
at his dead Grandpa

airport check-in …
a tantruming three-year-old
won't remove her shoes

beleaguered teen
withstanding a nonverbal
You're wearing *that*?

pre-Christmas ad ...
a pitchman explaining why
diamonds are love

severely burned man
relieved that his mother
is nearly blind

wedding reception ...
a dreadlocked Haitian singing
Cole Porter tunes

Kol Nidre service ...
Jewish boys trying to get
World Series updates

his four daughters
heading home from church
each on a cell phone

chemo patient smiles ~
her husband and adult sons
shaving their heads

two-year-old twins
in matching tuxedos
upstaging the bride

bus terminal …
tattooed, multi-pierced skinhead
solving Rubik's Cube

a day off from school …
Baptist girls celebrating
Rosh Hashanah

family photo …
their four children gazing
north, south, east, west

first trip to Brooklyn …
mistaking Hasidic Jews
for the Amish

post-liposuction
Dad requesting a pillow
for his Santa suit

faculty meeting …
observing a colleague
study his ear wax

grieving five-year-old
searching for the right shoe box
for his dead turtle

November 1st ...
Snickers and *Kit Kat* bars
in his breakfast bowl

Christmas morning ...
four elderly Jewish men
playing pinochle

mortified mother
passing gas audibly ...
her son's wedding

their three-year-old
trying on onion rings ...
breaded bracelets

April Fool's Day ...
stuffing a piñata
with egg salad

her three grandsons
standing upside-down,
their heads in buckets

elderly man
shaped like a question mark
asking why

Thanksgiving dinner ...
a vegan heart surgeon
carving grilled tuna

senile ex-sailor
painting his garage floor
aquamarine

newly licensed teen
trying to convince her Dad
she'll obey all limits

polygamist
recommending the practice
but for the in-laws

under their sofa
the father of three daughters
finds a blue condom

sweltering June day ...
beneath a cold shower,
singing *Jingle Bells*

centenarian
telling her eldest son
to button his coat

asking her rabbi
if one *Tic Tac* is a sin ~
Yom Kippur morning

physics professor
spit-polishing his wingtips
before commencement

hotel lobby ...
groom's Dad mistakes a bridesmaid
for a hooker

a hungry child
searching through a cupboard
she knows is empty

next-door neighbors
sending him via e-mail
Chanukah greetings

white supremacist
learning that his new grandson
has been named Jamal

birthday party ...
a haiku poet's daughters
turning five, seven

high school senior
asks his guidance counselor
about sheepherding

dropping her boyfriend
for agreeing with her Mom
regarding tattoos

shopping mall Santa ...
his long white beard covering
a Star of David

her three-year-old son
discovering a new use
for *Krazy Glue*

first day in prison …
he and his mammoth cellmate
getting acquainted

tenement mother
masking the holes in her walls
with finger-paintings

on the interstate …
the tongues of her son and dog
wag out the windows

depressed woman
grateful the winter solstice
has come and gone

three-pack-a-day man …
the smell of smoke precedes him
by several yards

her Jewish husband
introducing his in-laws
to a kasha knish

first night together ...
trying hard to ignore
her Pooh bedsheet

old New Yorker
insists on being buried
holding a cheesecake

his daughter ~ matching
the colors of her barrettes
and shoelaces

two eighty-year-olds
in motorized wheelchairs
drag racing

greasy spoon patron
requesting only egg whites
with his scrapple

interfaith couple ...
in their crèche, baby Jesus
wears a yarmulke

celiac patient
struggling to overcome
Entenmann's envy

his social worker
solemnly explaining why
she doesn't trust men

express lane purist
regarding a dozen eggs
as twelve items

In natural science, I have understood, there is nothing petty to the mind that has a large vision of relations, and to which every single object suggests a vast sum of conditions. It is surely the same with the observation of human life.

George Eliot

Bronx toll booth …
a savant memorizing
a Montana tag

ashen young man
observing his fiancée
purchase Limburger

a patient singing
Do You Hear What I Hear …
Christmas at Bellevue

wedding morning …
a very nervous groom
practicing *I do*

would-be writer
bemoaning there's nothing left
to be said

Chinese New Year …
the Chang family dining
at *Pastrami King*

Mormon patriarch
filling his new Rolodex
with grandchildren

British Bar Mitzvah …
a klezmer band taking on
The Rolling Stones

Christmas mass …
a Jewish guest is told
God *does* love him

out-of-town motel …
images from his wedding
keep intruding

It's a boy ...
first-time great-grandmother
requests a cigar

peewee football coach
making eighteen sandwiches,
all without crusts

nursing home supper ...
each man at the kids' table
is over sixty

bipolar teen ...
sleeping with a rope
under his mattress

after the nightmare
waking up to discover
he just hit his wife

his son resolves
to teach himself how to play
the bagpipes

commemorating
their first injury-free year ...
cheerleading squad

at 5 a.m.
searching for three solutions ...
yesterday's crosswords

pre-turkey dinner ...
four middle-aged brothers
remove their belts

Jewish boy asking
whether a football helmet
can be a skullcap

from the bathroom
his broken-handed father
calls for assistance

a man at the bank
requesting fifty dollars
in old pennies

crowded metro ...
reaching for the back pocket
of a well-dressed man

senryu writer
seeking a synonym ...
one less syllable

his three-year-old son
celebrates not falling down
even once that day

post-hurricane ...
searching for food, clothes,
blankets, meaning

before dining
an old man ties a napkin
around his dog's neck

seated in long rows
sewing American flags ...
female convicts

widow wondering
whether her late husbands
have met in heaven

Yom Kippur, midday ...
spotting a slice of brisket
in the men's room

teenager's father
reeling upon noticing
she has cleavage

his third wife
teaching him how to give
a compliment

four-year-old girl
buckling her baby brother
in her doll stroller

between clients
at the massage parlor
she calls her broker

remembering Mom
wearing ruby red lipstick,
kissing the air

sends back the soup
mistaking her false eyelash
for a mosquito

twin boys in the tub ...
gallons of displaced water
on their grandmother

police officer
asked by a four-year-old girl
to club her brother

blue jay squawking
above the home dugout ...
Oriole Park

tenement child
requests but one Christmas gift ...
a trampoline

job candidate
concluding each sentence
with a hollow laugh

Malibu teen
insists on purchasing
pre-ripped jeans

at *Kohl's*, an old man
smiling at a mannequin
in a wheelchair

travel agent
daydreaming of, one day,
boarding a plane

U.S. senator
uttering the word *frankly*
once too often

white-haired since '90
wondering if it's too late
to start coloring

adoptive father
hearing his Korean son
called a little Chink

psychoanalyst
searching on the internet
for the perfect couch

their son arguing
that a *desperate want*
equals a *need*

OCD child
rechecking the quality
of his pencil points

veteran teacher
congratulates a student
for sheer chutzpah

her homework untouched,
a twelve-year-old studying
movie star gossip

paperless poet
bemoaning the haiku
that slipped away

faculty retreat ...
noticing that three colleagues
have mismatched socks

a baby carriage
filled with clothes, pushed
by a homeless child

newspaper obit
providing no mention
of his first two wives

her gay uncle
giving a tutorial
on mascara

his new patient
contradicting herself twice
within three minutes

first-year resident
arguing with an old man
about cough drops

ten-month-old baby
and the family dachshund
chewing the same bone

alarming increase
in gravely ill relatives ...
final exam eve

psychotic Jew
calling a poinsettia
anti-Semitic

first day of school ...
saving her loudest tantrum
for the bus driver

inner city ...
between two gutted row homes
Mae's Beauty Salon

freshman's parents
pay a visit, bringing
meat, toilet paper

infirm old man
urging a sad-eyed child
to smile for him

her coloring book
filled with penguins crayoned
in pink, green, purple

internist's office ...
middle-aged woman asking
not to be weighed

on Thanksgiving
a bed-ridden child plucking
surgical-glove birds

senile ex-teacher
remembering each stanza
of *Paul Revere's Ride*

fearing stained teeth
she sips her espresso
through a straw

child therapist
telling his depressed wife
their son is her fault

geometry class ...
high school linebacker sketching
third-down formations

Jewish nine-year-old
wonders if Yiddish accents
come with age

French chef's children
preferring Hostess *Twinkies*
to his crème brûlée

I try to catch every sentence, every word you and I say, and quickly lock all these sentences and words away in my literary storehouse because they might come in handy.

Anton Chekhov

Bible class ...
a child asking how the deaf
hear God's voice

his blond daughter
asserting that Goldilocks
was misunderstood

New Year's Day ...
she resolves to sample
each *Breyers* flavor

Catholic schoolgirl
asking what should she do
to become a saint

in jail, realizing
three public library books
are overdue

twelve-year-old comic
trying out a new routine
in his Spanish class

demented woman ...
her son searching for life
in her dark blue eyes

family black sheep
declines attending the game
with his face painted

bored ninth grader
typing a book report
with his big toes

the Burns family
debating whether to name
their newborn, Forrest

dwarf brothers
newly wed to dwarf sisters
ponder their gene pool

quarterback shifting
from Abilene to Oxford
as a Rhodes Scholar

college term paper ...
its final sentence ends
with a smiley face

4'9" mother
trying to discipline teens
nearly twice her size

guidance counselor
calculating the seconds
left in the school year

first-year grad student
asking his research mentor
to co-sign a loan

psychotic twins
sharing hallucinations
and medications

a painter spackles
while trying hard to ignore
the wall's bullet holes

looking for his belt
her seven-year-old son
misplaces his pants

dermatologists
throwing a bachelor party
at a strip club

father-and-son talk
punctuated by Dad's sighs
and Junior's eye rolls

during his sermon
their esteemed rabbi flicking
dandruff from his beard

elderly surgeon
teaching the new residents
basic Yiddish

winter nose job ...
a child gives his snowman
a smaller carrot

first road test ...
swerving to avoid a cat,
hits a jaywalker

breast-feeding mother,
lactose-intolerant man
fighting over milk

Russian weightlifter
in his home gym, bench pressing
his father-in-law

porn actress
trying to decompress
at the library

atop Santa's lap
their four-year-old requesting
to become an elf

longtime waitress
doing career counseling
with the regulars

three-year-old boy
chiding his grandfather
about spitting

state spelling bee ...
a Catholic boy winning
with *mezuzah*

depressed dieter
choosing between sugar-free
and no-fat yogurts

lying in traction
a haiku poet longs
for a garden

a Jew makes peace,
sharing her soup recipes
with her Sikh in-law

truck stop restroom ...
spraying his deodorant
on a toilet seat

psychotherapist
daydreaming as his patient
describes a nightmare

prison inmate
touching his daughter's face
tattooed on his arm

driving instructor
claiming he does penance
with each student

masquerade party ...
a nun wearing a dashiki
over her habit

a cell phone rings ...
five female students reaching
for their handbags

city bakery ...
an old man swoons, smelling
newly cut rye bread

last-second shot ...
an irate coach insults
his hapless team

her son, looking pained
when offered a piece of fruit
for dessert

sick of footnotes
a scholar trying his hand
at poetry

NBA all-star …
his grandmother claiming
he stole her moves

college gymnast
docked one-tenth of a point
for foul language

beauty parlor …
three hair stylists stand outside
smoking cigarettes

immigrant's young son
listening to Mother Goose
with a Greek accent

his first grad student
sending him grade school photos
of her grandchildren

irate poet ...
his girlfriend couldn't care less
about syllables

his pre-teen daughters
watching a '30s film, awed
by the cars, clothes

first retirement check
drawing sadness from a man
who loved his job

new superhero
concerned that a red cape
might be too much

science teacher
describing mumps and measles
to clueless students

lymphoma patient
wondering why he bothered
with all those sit-ups

newly licensed,
her teenaged son insisting
on a Hummer

beleaguered father
sorting his daughters' boyfriends
by their addictions

an actuary
reassuring his brother
pre bungee jump

high school daredevil
skateboarding down a handrail ~
his parents praying

watching a porn film
a young man worrying why
he is not aroused

public golf course ...
a morbidly obese man
in a mesh T-shirt

off-Broadway ...
their eldest son doubling
as actor, usher

a two-year-old boy
holding a scoop of ice cream
in each unwashed hand

defensive tackle
questioned by a reporter
one-third his girth

a street mime
handing out business cards ...
completely blank

job interviewee ...
each fingernail painted
a different shade

sullen professor
breaks down saying goodbye
to his final class

Super Bowl eve ...
the star quarterback waiting
for a manicure

five-year-old hunter
shooting at a snake disguised
as a jump rope

Reality

Their parents have heard
well-meaning friends, teachers,
and television characters
preaching to their children that
they can be anything they want to be
as long as they are passionate,
as long as they give it their all,
as long as they believe in themselves.

But—for the mentally retarded boy
who dreams of being a surgeon;
for the short, clumsy adolescent
longing to be an Olympic athlete;
for the child with palsy who aspires
to be a star of stage and screen—
their parents know better.

a colleague asking
where's the psychology
in senryu

army private
carving his daughter's name
inside his helmet

construction worker ...
salt and pepper shakers
in his lunchbox

an errant pass
felling a knight on horseback ...
other team's mascot

four-year-old Jew
musing if cow-shaped crackers
are meat or dairy

young academic
eschewing *PowerPoint*
opts for chalk

nudist beach ...
realizing that most folks
should remain clothed

Boston professor
visiting Tulane, adopts
a Cajun accent

pro athlete
looking for the right earrings
to match his suit

dining out, her son
requests two slices of bread ~
one toasted, one not

to his priest
a judge admits cheating
in fifth grade civics

a revered rabbi
stands on his icy driveway
sprinkling kosher salt

thirty years after
his missed field goal, the kicker
still hearing *Wide right*

a drunk driver
quoting Dylan Thomas
to an unmoved cop

on line at *Starbucks*
an old man asks his grandchild
how much for just black

her spell-checker
not correcting *genital*
mistyped for *gentle*

their son ponders why
Lincoln's birthday is honored
with mattress sales

interfaith council ...
a Methodist offering
the first *oy*

holding a walker
the bride's grandmother leads
a conga line

last day of work ...
a temp stuffing her pockets
with floppy disks

a Christian teen
affixing a Jesus fish
to his bicycle

just before show time
an aging rock star sharing
his eyeliner

esteemed professor
racing to a lab meeting
on his new skateboard

an old Jew
enraged that his grandson
bought an *Audi*

college open house ...
his daughter scrutinizing
the dorm bathrooms

shaving his head
hoping to look like Kojak,
gets Curley Howard

with his great-grandson
watching for the first time
The Wizard of Oz

doctor's waiting room ...
his wife sharing her symptoms
with complete strangers

corrupt CEO
wearing a three-piece white suit
to his arraignment

Chinese restaurant ...
she asks to replace wontons
with matzo balls

at midnight
their son wishing on a star
to be eight feet tall

blocked haiku poet
convinced that his muse
has moved to Iraq

at Penn Station
an Auschwitz survivor
suffering flashbacks

sending his sons
an e-mail from abroad ...
Obey Mom

old woman's hair ...
at least two shades darker
than her granddaughters'

depressed sushi chef
feels only his showmanship
elicits praise

in circuit court
his lawyer jotting down
a grocery list

third grade recital ...
a father in the back row
practicing card tricks

her boyfriend
responding to *I love you*
with *How come?*

post-collagen ...
her lush new lips holding
a cigarette

The folly of mistaking a paradox for a discovery, a metaphor for a proof, a torrent of verbiage for a spring of capital truths, and oneself for an oracle, is inborn in us.

Paul Valéry

Manifest plainness,
Embrace simplicity …

Lao-tzu

technical writer
thrilled to learn that his work
is considered prose

the groom's Dad, irate
about the bride's religion
and the cash bar

a sleepless playwright
wishing that his characters
would stop talking

Russian grad students
bemused by the concept
smoke-free area

a Greek tragedy
performed by high school actors
evoking laughter

first time in his home
she wonders why the bathroom
has no door

clueless young man
trying to pick up women ...
lesbian concert

college reunion ...
ex-Marxists describing
their summer homes

bibliophile
requesting to be buried
with *Don Quixote*

compulsive gambler
at his daughter's spelling bee
offering odds

burned-out physician
wishing he had majored
in modern dance

a Christmas letter
praising his brother's children ...
on the floor, crumpled

at an ATM
the old lady behind him
standing far too close

a large cardboard box
attracting three preschoolers
away from their toys

married two weeks
asking him for the first time
Do I look fat?

married two weeks
answering for the last time
Yes, you do look fat

Oscar night …
screenplay winner thanking
his old typewriter

Tae Kwon Do student
asks if he could simply buy
the black belt

moving out …
his son sitting on the curb,
pleads with him to stay

in gym class
a child doing push-ups,
bends only her toes

in her prom dress
discovering the power
of a bosom

novelist's mother
urging him to dedicate
his next book to her

an obese girl
on the South Beach diet
dreaming of éclairs

9 a.m. at school ...
mortifies his third grader
bringing in her lunch

grand opening ...
a laundrette/music store called
The Soap Opera

his fiancée
refusing to ingest food
touched by Styrofoam

Jim Lane, Ann Cates
learning their parents were born
Levy and Cohen

Little Italy ...
their son asking if iced tea
goes with veal

five-year-old sister
handing the crying baby
their mother's photo

a weary father
begging his teenaged daughter
to spare the drama

after the flood ...
a toddler's shoe bobbing
in a mud puddle

awaiting trial
three white-collar criminals
trading lawyer jokes

her great-grandfather
attributing his long life
to fast food

a businessman
rues his latest investment ...
Goldberg's Bar & Grill

post beauty pageant ...
the relieved winner gorging
on French fries

spotting a rat ~
an hysterical mother,
an intrigued child

a man's double chin
concealing nearly one-half
of his Windsor knot

a sick four-year-old
handing a tearful nurse
his chocolate milk

fifth grade English class
regarding proper grammar
as its enemy

Halloween prankster
giving trick-or-treaters
canned vegetables

faculty lounge ...
grad students and janitors
watch the Super Bowl

middle school loner
wishing that all his classmates
were as sad as he

their kindergartner
requesting a rhinestone leash
for her iguana

workaholic
uncertain of the names
of his grandchildren

their daughter's boyfriend
wearing white painter's pants
to her Bat Mitzvah

in a wordless rage
her musically challenged son
kicking his cello

trying to recall
when her husband's quirks
ceased being cute

high school reunion ...
the class nerds describing
how they got rich

at a garage sale
purchasing a power tie
for fifty cents

a toddler shrieking
as her Dad tries to discern:
fear, pain, or delight?

Boston, mid-winter ...
two homeless men discussing
global warming

college film students
watching a John Wayne western
rooting for Cochise

on his birthday
a demented man wishing
for baby sisters

New Year's evening ...
breaking their resolutions
between bowl games

pierced, tattooed teen
explaining to his mother
how he's evolving

Index of Poems' Original Sources

Some of the poems presented in *Specks and Flashes* have been published or are "in press" elsewhere. Listed below are the titles of these poems and the journals in which they have appeared or soon will appear.

In **Haiku Headlines:** *ex-ballerina; family photo; Fenway in April; funeral parlor; seventh heaven; two-year-old twins*
In **Modern Haiku:** *faculty meeting; New Year's evening*
In **The Pegasus Review:** *elderly man; her three-year-old son*

Author's Note

Dr. Robert H. Deluty has been a psychology professor at the University of Maryland, Baltimore County since 1980. He was named UMBC's Presidential Teaching Professor in 2002 and is currently the Director of the Clinical Psychology Doctoral Program. Born and raised in New York City, he now lives in Ellicott City, Maryland with his wife, Barbara, and their children, Laura and David. *Specks and Flashes* is his eighth book.